ALIENS STOLE MY
UNDERPANTS
AND OTHER INTERGALACTIC POEMS

Brian Moses lives in Sussex with his wife and two daughters. He travels the country presenting his poems in schools and libraries. He is keen to perform his poems to all kinds of beings on different planets, providing that they pay his travel expenses and promise not to keep him there for scientific research purposes!

Lucy Maddison lives in Balham, south London, with her partner Brian, daughter Sami and Jess the cat.

ALIENS STOLE MY UNDERPANTS
AND OTHER INTERGALACTIC POEMS

Chosen by Brian Moses

Illustrated by Lucy Maddison

MACMILLAN CHILDREN'S BOOKS

*For Susie, Gaby and Lesley –
an intergalactic trio!*

Aliens Stole My Underpants and Other Intergalactic Poems
First published 1998 by Macmillan Children's Books
Aliens Stole My Underpants 2
First published 2001 by Macmillan Children's Books

This omnibus edition published 2005 by Macmillan Children's Books
a division of Macmillan Publishers Ltd
20 New Wharf Road, London N1 9RR
Basingstoke and Oxford
Associated companies throughout the world
www.panmacmillan.com

ISBN 978-0-330-43874-2

A CIP catalogue record for this book is available from the British Library.

Printed and bound in Great Britain by Mackays of Chatham plc, Chatham, Kent.

'On Some Other Planet' and 'Rockets and Quasars' by John Rice were first published in
Rockets and Quasars by Aten Press 1984.
'The Blob' by Wes Magee was first published in *The Witch's Brew and other poems* by
Cambridge University Press 1989.
'Aliens on Vacation' from *Wish You Were Here (And I Wasn't)*. Text and illustration © 1999
Colin McNaughton. Reproduced by permission of the publisher,
Walker Books Ltd, London.
The poem 'The Alien Barbecues' by Brian Moses was especially written for BBC Schools
Online and features many of the 'favourite words' that children emailed to the site.

CONTENTS

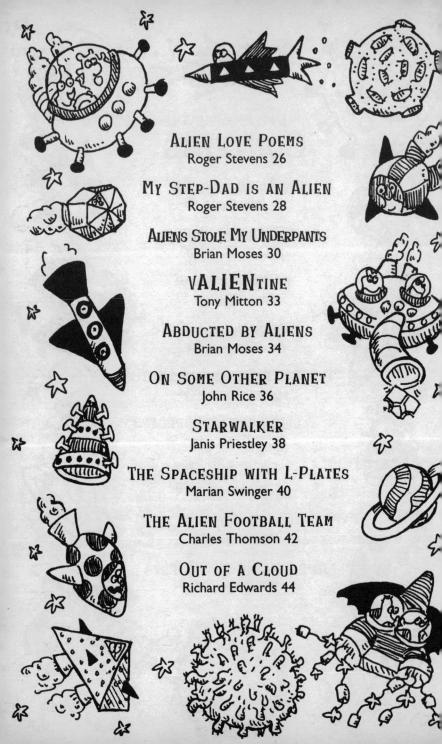

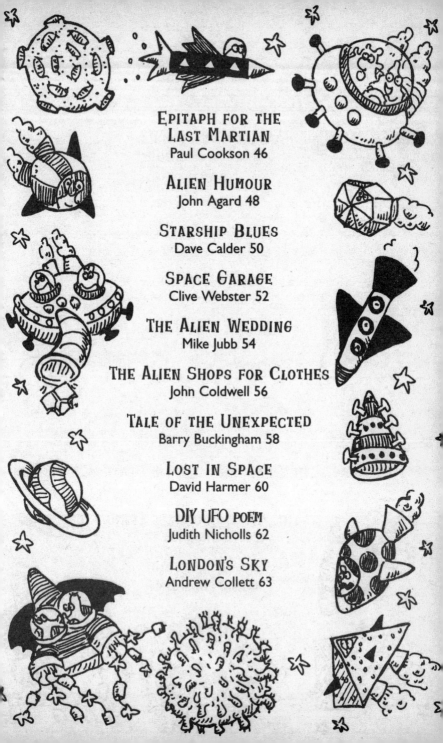

ROCKETS AND QUASARS

Rockets and quasars,
planets and stars,
I'm fed up with Earth
. . . so I'll see you on Mars!!

John Rice

NEW KID AT SCHOOL

Last term we got a new kid at school.
Turned out to be a boy but we weren't sure at first.
It's difficult to tell when all the family have
green spotty skin, moustaches and eyes on stalks.

His name was 2£Bzz6gnnfqurjh.
Trouble was, no one could pronounce it properly,
even he couldn't, so he got nicknamed Clunk instead.

Clunk soon became popular in our class.
For one thing he was good at maths
and used to help us with our homework.
'Right, what's 4000 x 3.619 + 28.5 ÷ by the square root
    of 729?'
He'd press his nostril (the third on the left),
there'd be a bleep in his shirt
and a piece of paper would come out of his neck that
    said '537.2037037'.

He was so powerful he could even make school dinners
taste really nice with a click of his fingers
– all twenty-six of them.
Sparks would fly and with a zoom and a ping
cabbage would turn into ice cream
and sausages into chocolate bars.

Clunk was the sports day champion.
He broke the record for the 100m . . . 2.4 seconds,
won the three-legged race by himself
and then subdivided himself to the power of four
to win the relay
before sending the javelin, shot, discus and sandpit
into orbit with just one throw.
(It was on the news later that these items had been
photographed as UFOs and then hit twelve planes, three
helicopters and a hang-glider from Worksop.)

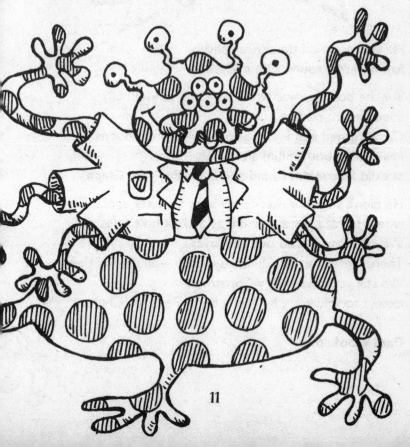

He was great on the school photo,
had his arms round all our class.

But the best day was when Hulk the school bully
tried to pick on him.
Clunk turned him into a poodle with pink ribbons.
Hulk didn't bother him after that,
but did follow him round asking for Pedigree Chum.

He didn't stay long, had to go back to outer space
where his dad got a new job as a black hole salesman.
We cried as we said our goodbyes.
There were tears in Clunk's eyes too – all nine of them.
We still get cards every Christmas,
except for Hulk . . . he gets a tin of Pedigree Chum.

Paul Cookson

THE YAFFLING YAHOO

A do-it-yourself space-rhyme

The Yaffling Yahoo
is a silly blue moo
but when she feels mean
she turns a bright . . . . . .

She shrinks herself small
when dry rain starts to fall.
She's an ugly disgrace
with those splumps on her . . . . . .

She enjoys a long drink
from a tank of pink ink,
then will sprint down the street
on her twelve pairs of . . . . . .

When her back gets an itch
then her nose starts to twitch.
She is skyscraper tall
yet as round as a . . . . . .

The Yaffling Yahoo
just hasn't a clue.
She continues to chase
through the dark depths of . . . . . .

Wes Magee

ALIEN EXCHANGE

We've got an alien at our school
he's on an exchange trip
I'd quite fancy him
if he wasn't so weird looking.
Just one head
only two legs
and no feelers at all
he hasn't got claws on the end of his hands
and he's only got – don't laugh - two eyes.

Can you believe that?
When we first saw him we fell about
but as our teacher says
we must be thoughtful and respect all visitors
to our galaxy
even if they have got only one feeding system
a breathing tube that is much too small
and horrid furry stuff on their head.

Next month my sister and I
are visiting his planet on the exchange.
It's got a funny name, Earth.
We've got to stay two weeks
our teacher says we must be careful
not to tread on the Earthlings by mistake
and always, always be polite
to raise our wings in greeting
and to put rubber tips on our sharpest horns.
I'm not looking forward to it much
the food looks awful
and the sea's dirty, not to mention the air.
Still, it'll make a change from boring old school
and perhaps some alien
will quite fancy me!

David Harmer

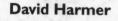

THE ALIEN TEACHER

Each night, Mr Potiphar peeled off his face
and commuted by rocket to outermost space.
Returning each morning, he screwed back his eyes
and reduced his antennae to minimum size.
Inserting his lungs, he would deeply inhale
while removing his gill flaps and shedding his tail.
After casting his skin with a writhe and a jerk,
he would dress himself smartly and drive off to work.
He worked as a teacher. The Head was no fool.
She employed only aliens to teach at her school.
'They are better than Earthlings,' I heard her remark.
'They have far larger brains and can see in the dark
and the pupils get day trips to Luna or Mars
and sightseeing jaunts to the furthermost stars.
They're developing talents like reading the mind,
teleportation and things of that kind,
and (the Head quivered with ill-restrained mirth)
we plan in due course, to take over the Earth.'

Marian Swinger

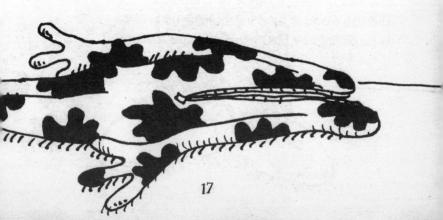

ELVIS IS BACK!

Rumours persist in the press that the rock singer Elvis Presley faked his death. One of the most bizarre ideas is that Elvis was in touch with aliens and that they came down to Earth to spirit him away! One day, of course, he may decide to stage a comeback!

When aliens brought Elvis Presley back
it looked as if we were under attack
as a mother ship of incredible size
sank down to Earth right in front of our eyes,
and it really gave us an almighty shock
when out of its doors stepped the King of Rock.

There was laughter, tears and celebration,
Elvis is back, he's been on vacation.
There he stood looking leaner and fitter,
Elvis is back, in a suit made of glitter.
It seems the doubters were right all along,
Elvis is back with a dozen new songs.

He's been cutting an album somewhere in space,
now he's bringing it home to the human race.
And the world is listening, holding its breath,
to recordings by Elvis made after his 'death'.

And of course he'd duped us all into thinking
it was pills and burgers and too much drinking
that killed him off, but that wasn't the case,
Elvis escaped to a different place.
He's been touring out there, a star upon stars,
rocking the universe, Venus to Mars.

And as alien ships descend from above
we're sending out our message of love
and hoping they'll show no desire to attack,
but we don't really care because ELVIS IS BACK!

Brian Moses

DEAR ALIEN

I newly learn your Earth-Speak –
forgive if I get it wrong.
When I don't know the Earth-word
I shall have to write in *Sprong*.

Sorry to start 'Dear Alien',
but now our planets are twinned,
I hope as we get to know each other
we shall want to write 'Dear *fribble*'.

I am thirty-two, in *Sprong*-years;
in Earth-years, I'd be eight.
My mum's one-hundred-and-twenty today
so we're going to celebrate.

She's invited us all to a *poggle*,
and baked a birthday cake,
with a hundred and twenty *clabbits* on top.
(Is my Earth-speak without a mistake?)

Me, please, to tell what I wrong get,
my lovely new pen-*fribble*.
I want to learn all about Earth.
Write and tell me all your *gribble*.

I shall now tell you what I look like:
my hair is short and red
on my arms and legs, and greenish-*grump*
and curly on my head.

My *ecklings* are blue and yellow,
with the middle one black and white.
I'm told that Earthlings have only two –
can you really see all right?

I have a brother and sister,
and a lovely pet *splink* called Bloggs.
Is it true you have pets with four legs and a tail?
What do you call them – *droggs*?

Please write back soon, dear Earthling,
don't keep me waiting long –
and remember to tell me your Earth-words
that, today, I've written in *Sprong*.

Celia Warren

THE BLOB

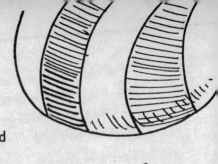

And . . . what is it like?

> Oh, it's scary and fatbumped
> and spike-eared and groany.
> It's hairy and face-splumped
> and bolshy and bony.

And . . . where does it live?

> Oh, in comets and spaceships
> and pulsars and black holes.
> In craters and sheepdips
> and caverns and north poles.

And . . . what does it eat?

> Oh, roast rocks and fishlegs
> and X-rays and mooncrust.
> Then steelmeat and sun-eggs
> and lava and spacedust.

And . . . who are its enemies?

Oh, Zonkers and Moonquakes
and Sunquarks and Zigbags.
Dumb Duncers and Milkshakes
and Smogsters and Wigwags.

And . . . and . . . what does it wear?

Not a thing!
It's bare!

Wes Magee

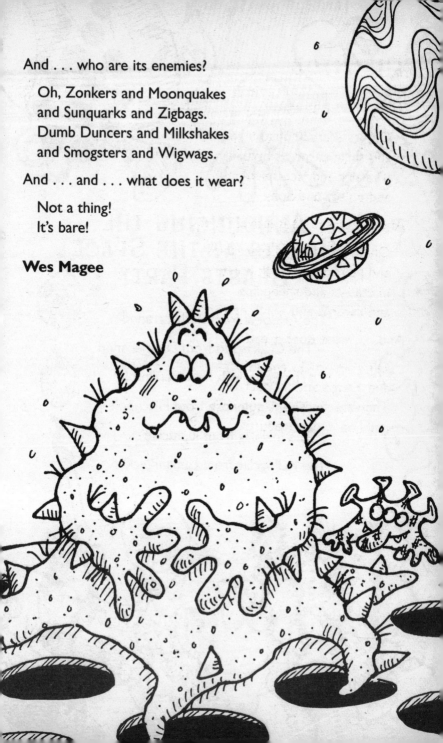

ANNOUNCING THE GUESTS AT THE SPACE BEASTS' PARTY

'The Araspew from Bashergrannd'

'The Cakkaspoo from Danglebannd'

'The Eggisplosh from Ferrintole'

'The Gurglenosh from Hiccupole'

'The Inkiblag from Jupitickle'

'The Kellogclag from Lamandpickle'

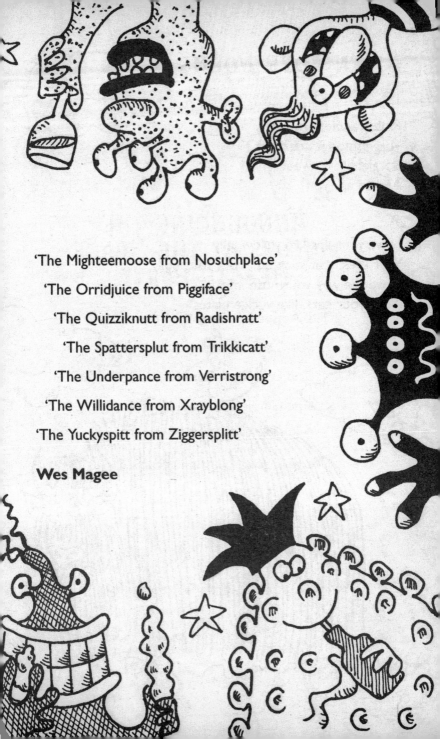

'The Mighteemoose from Nosuchplace'

'The Orridjuice from Piggiface'

'The Quizziknutt from Radishratt'

'The Spattersplut from Trikkicatt'

'The Underpance from Verristrong'

'The Willidance from Xrayblong'

'The Yuckyspitt from Ziggersplitt'

Wes Magee

ALIEN LOVE POEMS

1
Ribblerabbles are red
Vorglesmoogs are blue
Borglemilk is sweet
And so are you

2
I love your lips like yellow jelly
Your eyes, that stick out from your belly
I love the way your nose inflates
I love your ears, like vuckle plates

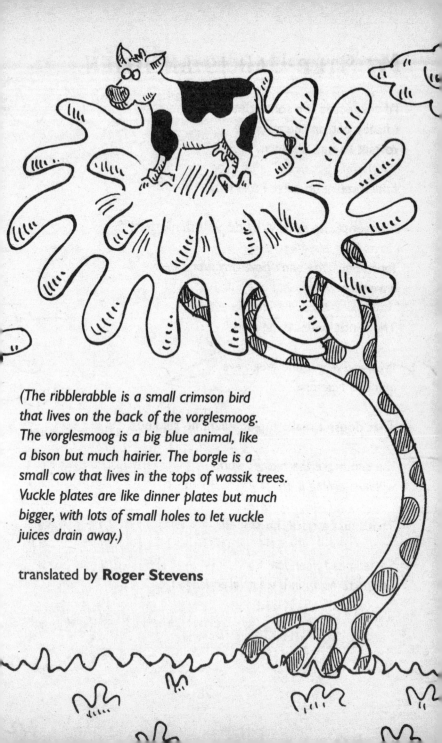

(The ribblerabble is a small crimson bird
that lives on the back of the vorglesmoog.
The vorglesmoog is a big blue animal, like
a bison but much hairier. The borgle is a
small cow that lives in the tops of wassik trees.
Vuckle plates are like dinner plates but much
bigger, with lots of small holes to let vuckle
juices drain away.)

translated by **Roger Stevens**

MY STEP-DAD IS AN ALIEN

I'd suspected for some time.
I finally got up the courage
to talk to him about it.

I think you're an alien, I told him.

Nonsense, he said. Why do you think that?

*You're bald. You don't have any hair
anywhere.*

That's not unusual, he said.

*Well, you've got one green eye
and one blue one.*

That doesn't make me an alien, he replied.

*You can make the toaster work
without turning it on.*

That's just a trick, he smiled.

*Sometimes I hear you
talking to Mum in a weird alien language.*

I'm learning Greek
and Mum lets me practise on her.

What about your bright blue tail?

Ah, he said thoughtfully.
You're right, of course.
So, the tail gave it away, did it?

Roger Stevens

ALIENS STOLE MY UNDERPANTS

To understand the ways
of alien beings is hard,
and I've never worked it out
why they landed in my backyard.

And I've always wondered why
on their journey from the stars,
these aliens stole my underpants
and took them back to Mars.

They came on a Monday night
when the weekend wash had been done,
pegged out on the line
to be dried by the morning sun.

Mrs Driver from next door
was a witness at the scene
when aliens snatched my underpants —
I'm glad that they were clean!

It seems they were quite choosy
as nothing else was taken.
Do aliens wear underpants
or were they just mistaken?

I think I have a theory
as to what they wanted them for,
they needed to block off a draught
blowing in through the spacecraft door.

Or maybe some Mars museum
wanted items brought back from space.
Just think, my pair of Y-fronts
displayed in their own glass case.

And on the label beneath
would be written where they got 'em
and how such funny underwear
once covered an Earthling's bottom!

Brian Moses

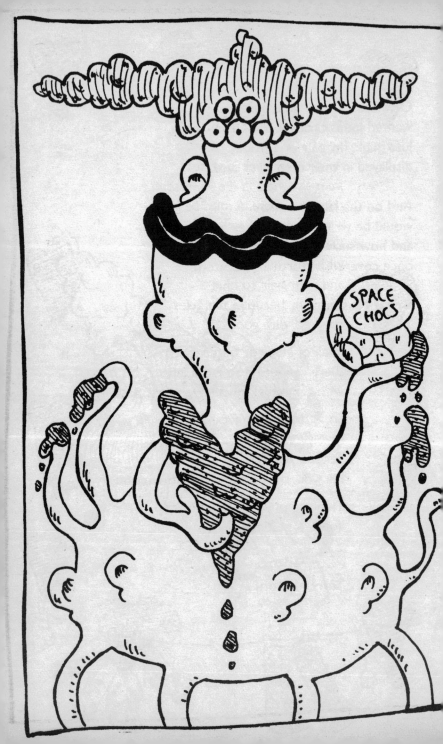

vALIENtine

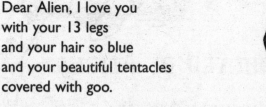

An alien valentine in verse
from elsewhere in the universe.
(Heavens above. It must be love.)

Dear Alien, I love you
with your 13 legs
and your hair so blue
and your beautiful tentacles
covered with goo.

In all of inner or outer space
there cannot be so fair a face
with ears stuck on all over the place.

So let me be your satellite
revolving round you every night.
Tell me yes. Ah, tell me soon.
For you, my dear, I'm over the moon.

Thinking of you, I cannot sleep.
Yours X-static-ly,
                    E.T. BLEEP

Tony Mitton

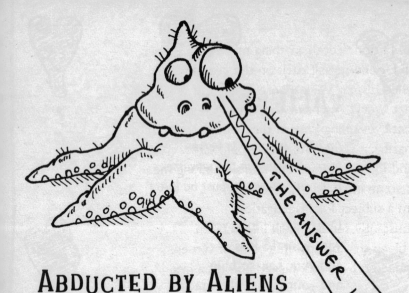

THE ANSWER IS

ABDUCTED BY ALIENS

When Jack came back to school
after one day's absence, unexplained,
he went and told his teacher
he'd been abducted by aliens.
She told him not to be so daft,
but he gave us all the details –
what the spacecraft had looked like,
how extra-terrestrials kidnapped him
then carried him onto their ship.
And Jack told his story
again and again. 'When they landed,' he said,
'I was terrified, couldn't move,
I nearly died, then a blade of light
cut the night in two, trapped me
in its beam so I couldn't see. I felt
arms that were rubbery wrapped around me,
like the coils of our garden hose.

And I don't recall anything more
till I found myself back on the ground
while rasping voices were telling me
that everything I saw they would see,
that everything I heard they would hear,
that everything I ate they would taste.
And I know they're out there watching me,
in some intergalactic laboratory.
I'm a subject for investigation
constantly sending back information,
a bleep that bleeps on a bank of screens,
abducted by aliens, tagged and then freed.'

'What nonsense you talk,' his teacher said.
'Take out your books, who's ready for maths?'
But Jack couldn't make his figures come right.
If communication works both ways, he thought,
then he might benefit too –
maybe aliens could help solve his multiplication!

Brian Moses

ON SOME OTHER PLANET

On some other planet
near some other star,
there's a music-loving alien
who drives a blue car.

On some other planet
on some far distant world,
ther's a bright sunny garden
where a cat lies curled.

On some other planet
a trillion miles away,
there are parks and beaches
where the young aliens play.

On some other planet
in another time-zone,
there are intelligent beings
who feel very much alone.

On some other planet
one that we can't see,
there must be one person
who's a duplicate of me.

John Rice

STARWALKER

My cat's an extra-terrestrial.
He walks the stars at night.
He plants one paw on Betelgeuse
for it is his by right.

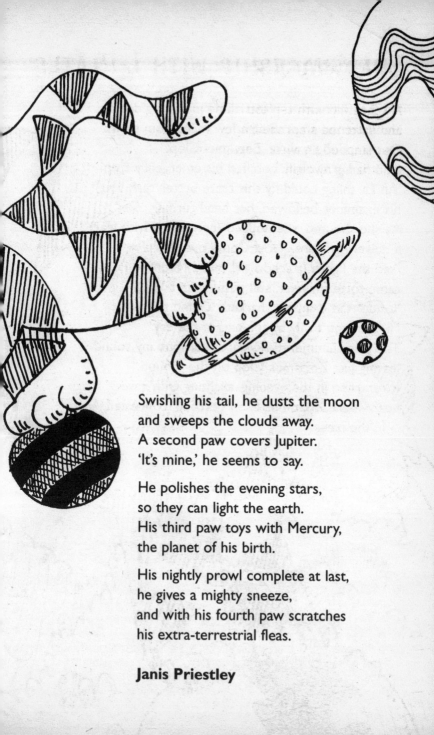

Swishing his tail, he dusts the moon
and sweeps the clouds away.
A second paw covers Jupiter.
'It's mine,' he seems to say.

He polishes the evening stars,
so they can light the earth.
His third paw toys with Mercury,
the planet of his birth.

His nightly prowl complete at last,
he gives a mighty sneeze,
and with his fourth paw scratches
his extra-terrestrial fleas.

Janis Priestley

THE SPACESHIP WITH L-PLATES

A spaceship with L-plates came juddering down
and flattened a cornfield a few miles from town.
Out stepped an alien, Zozzimus Glop,
who had grievously botched his emergency stop.
'An Earthling could fly this crate better than you,'
his examiner bellowed, her head turning blue.
As she shouted, she noticed (congealing with fear)
a quivering figure. 'Hoy! Come over here.'
And the figure (a schoolgirl called Madeline Pike)
came tottering over, still pushing its bike.
'Inside,' the examiner barked. 'Come this way.
I'll train you to fly by the end of the day.'
The ship shimmered skywards without any sound
leaving just Zozzimus Glop on the ground.
It returned in the evening, alighting with ease
near where Zozzimus Glop perched, concealed,
    in the trees.

The examiner shouted, 'Glop. Come here you fool.
This Earthling, as soon as she's finished with school,
will be training with us on our starship in space.'
Zozzimus slouched to the ship in disgrace.
But future commander, proud Madeline Pike,
gave a salute and went home on her bike.

Marian Swinger

THE ALIEN FOOTBALL TEAM

I'm in the alien football team.
All of us have five feet.
We run at a hundred miles an hour.
We're the team no one can beat.

We don't need to shout to get the ball –
we're telepathic instead.
We've got X-ray vision to see through defenders
and eyes in the back of our head.

We haven't ever bought a transfer
and I'm sure we never will.
How could you ever improve a team
that usually wins ninety–nil!

We've won the double double double
dozens of years on the run.
The trouble is that winning so easily
really isn't much fun.

You'd think an unbroken record like ours
was the ideal one to choose,
but we get so bored. How nice it would be,
just even once, to lose.

Charles Thomson

OUT OF A CLOUD

I have never seen one,
Desmond saw one though,
He said it hummed like hives of bees,
He said it glowed a glow,
He said it swooped out of a cloud
And lit the fields below,
He said it took his heart away,
Desmond's UFO.

Of course no one believed him,
But wandering here and there,
Desmond scanned the sky each night
With his hopeful stare,
Examining the Milky Way,
Venus, the Plough, the Bear,
Searching, wishing, longing,
Desmond head-in-air.

And then, one day, he vanished.
How? We'll never know.
We found no clue or trace of him,
Hunting high and low,
Except, spiked on a barbed-wire fence,
A note saying: 'Told you so,'
And all around the grass pressed down . . .
Where did Desmond go?

Richard Edwards

EPITAPH FOR THE LAST MARTIAN

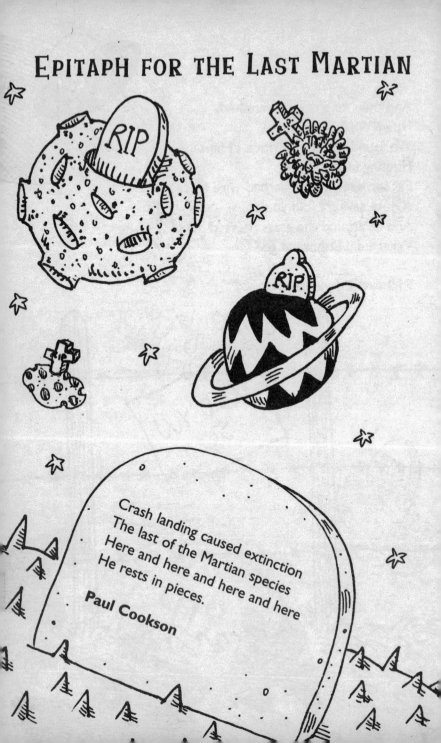

Crash landing caused extinction
The last of the Martian species
Here and here and here and here
He rests in pieces.

Paul Cookson

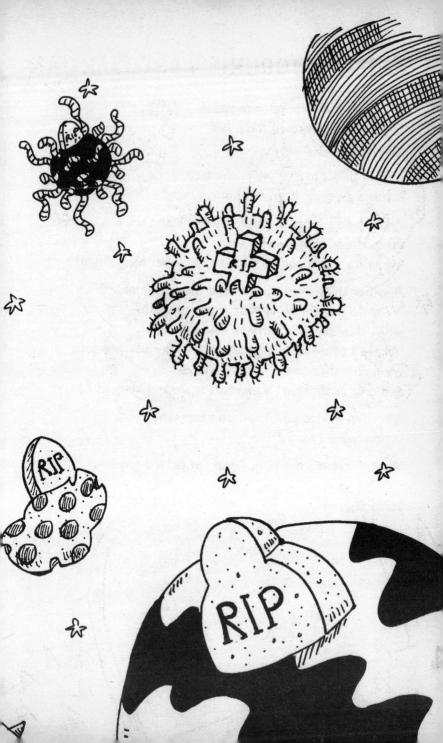

ALIEN HUMOUR

A visiting alien from out of space
could not understand the jokes
that Earthlings make.

'When they throw a pie in the face,
is this a greeting from the human race?

And why do most Earthling comics stand up,'
asked the alien with a frown,
'when it's more comfortable to tell jokes lying down?

Another thing I've noticed,' said the alien amazed.
'Why do you throw eggs at your politicians
when they say things that make you angry?
Where I come from eggs are so wonderfully precious
we throw them only on festive days
and only at those who make us smile and keep us happy.'

'Well I'm tickled pink,' said one Earthling.
'Know what I mean?'

'Maybe,' replied the alien. 'And I'm tickled green.'

John Agard

STARSHIP BLUES

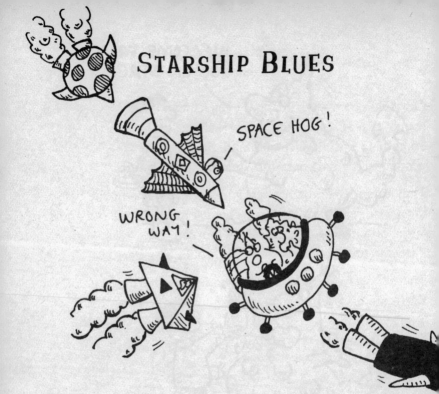

It's hard out on a spaceship, couldn't get much worse,
All we get to see is the same old universe.

The food tastes like rubber and looks like concrete tiles
We only change our spacesuits every million million miles
The captain's going crazy, he thinks we're crocodiles
The doctor's seeing double, the atomic drive's got piles.

We've been light years in a rocket-jam on the Milky Way
It's 'Watch that star!' and 'Mind that sun!' all day
We never get back home, we never see our pay
The ones we left behind have all turned old and grey.

Our ship's computer's happy, it thinks it's made of cheese
It only answers questions put in ancient Japanese
Something with no face and a horrible disease
is doing something nasty down in the deep-freeze.

They told us we'd be heroes, go where none had gone before
but we sit and stare at starscreens till our eyes are red and sore
Sirius or Saturn, I don't care any more,
if it wasn't for the black holes life would be a bore.

There's a jelly in my cabin, it's eaten up my berth
Beam me up, beam me down, beam me back to earth.

Dave Calder

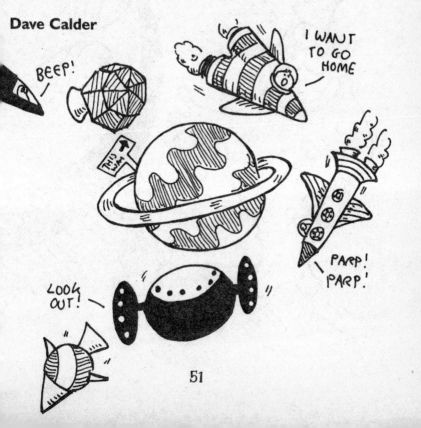

51

SPACE GARAGE

The garage for second-hand spaceships
Was trying to sell off its stock.
They advertised, 'One careful owner,
Only one billion miles on the clock ...'

Clive Webster

THE ALIEN WEDDING

When the aliens got married,
The bride was dressed in zeet;
And with a flumzel in her groyt,
She really looked a treat.

The groom was onggy spoodle,
He felt a little quenz;
The best man told him not to cronk
In front of all their friends.

The bride's ensloshid father
Had slupped down too much glorter;
He grobbled up the aisle alone,
Then flomped back for his daughter.

The lushen bridesmaids followed
With such wigantic walks;
Their optikacious oggers
Were sparkling on their stalks.

The bride and groom entroathed their splice,
They swapped a little squip;
Then he splodged her on the kisser,
And she flimped him on the blip.

And after the wedding breakfast,
The stroadling and the laughter,
The loving pair took off to Mars,
And splayed winkerly ever after.

Mike Jubb

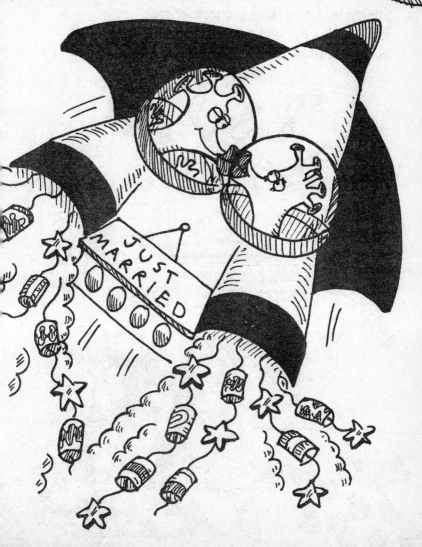

THE ALIEN SHOPS FOR CLOTHES

The alien raised a tentacle and opened the door
Of a famous London fashion store
He glanced at the jackets on the smart suit rail,
Checked out the sweaters in the half-price sale.
He ran his trunk along the trouser rack
Picked out a pair and put them back.
He flicked through the socks with his one blue claw,

He sniffed the T-shirts and began to roar,
'I wanted something casual, off the peg.
Denim or cotton with just the one leg.'
The alien rolled his three red eyes.
'But you don't stock anything in my size.
And another thing, before I leave
Your sweaters all need an extra sleeve.
The Spring Collection is a total disgrace,
It only caters for the human race!'
He oozed from the store and hailed a taxi
And did the rest of his shopping in another galaxy.

John Coldwell

TALE OF THE UNEXPECTED

The Martians are a-coming –
they're running down the street.
Their blasters are a-gleaming,
and there's red dust on their feet.

Terrestrials scitter-scatter,
for there's panic all about.
Pink Martian eyes are goggling;
purple tongues flick in and out.

What brings these aliens Earthwards?
No, it isn't what you think.
They've just popped down for fish and chips,
and a can of fizzy drink.

Barry Buckingham

LOST IN SPACE

When the spaceship first landed
nose down in Dad's prize vegetables
I wasn't expecting the pilot
to be a large blue blob with seven heads
the size and shape of rugby balls
and a toothy grin on his fourteen mouths.

'Is this Space Base Six?' he asked.
'No,' I said, 'it's our back garden, number fifty-two.'
'Oh,' he said, 'are you sure?'
and took from his silver overalls
a shiny book of maps.

There were routes round all the galaxies
ways to the stars through deepest space
maps to planets I'd never heard of
maps to comets, maps to moons
and short cuts to the sun.

'Of course,' he said, 'silly me,
I turned right, not left, at Venus,
easily done, goodbye.'
He shook his heads, climbed inside,
the spaceship roared into the sky
and in a shower of leeks and cabbages
disappeared for ever.

David Harmer

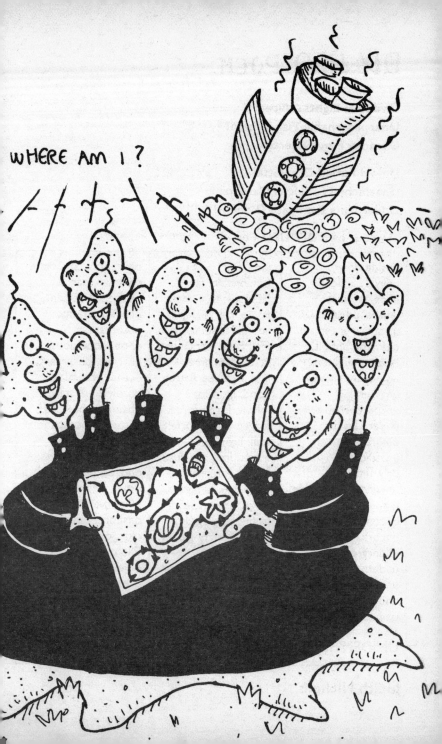

DIY UFO Poem

Umbrella Fights Officer?
Unapproachable Fish Offside?
Uncanny Frog Objects?

Unfold Furled Omelette?
Unattached Fabulous Oarsman?
Underpants Fumigate Oldham?

Try your own DIY UFO Poem!

upside down, unlikely, unload, underground, united, uncle, uncanny, uncertain, ultimate, unbolt, Hugh, unbeaten, unbutton, unaware, unassuming, unapproachable, under, unable, umbrella, under, unattached, ugly, ultimate, unwind, unscramble, unmentionable, unconscious, uncork, unlikely, underground, underpants, undeveloped, understand, unfold, unique . . .	fade, fish, fashionable, fabric, fabulous, face, facts, fiddle, fail, fair/fare, fat, fall, false, fame, feel, faint, ferocious, fit, fill, film, fine, find, fix, first, flatten, flood, fly, fume, follow, foggy, force, forget, forge, forfeit, foul, fighting, free, fritter, frog, fry, fuse, funnel, futuristic, fuzzy, fun, fumigate, frolic, front, friendly, frequently, frizzle, first, flibberty-gibbet, formidable, form, forlorn, foreign, first, French, foreboding, foolish, fraudulent . . .	obligation, oak, oath, oarsman, oar, oatmeal, obedient, obelisk, obesity, observation, oboe, obnoxious, obscure, observant, ocean, obsession, obsolete, obstacle, obstinacy, obvious, occasion, occupation, office, occupant, October, octuplets, odd, oddball, ode, other, offence, offer, official, offside, offshore, offspring, okay, okapi, oil, Oldham, Olympic, omelette, one-stop, ozone, opposite, onomatopoeia, ooze, outrageous . . .
UNIDENTIFIED	FLYING	OBJECT

Judith Nicholls

LONDON'S SKY

A UFO came speeding
in the dead of night,
turned left at the pillar-box
then first right.

Shooting down the high street
lighting London's sky,
a giant, marshmallow shape;
one overgrown pork pie.

And slowing down a little,
as out jumped tiny men,
green and yellow, just one eye,
all heading for Big Ben.

Sliding down its towers,
across its moonlit face
to set their watches one more time
before shooting back to space.

Andrew Collett

ALIENS STOLE MY UNDERPANTS 2

THEY'RE BACK! MORE INTERGALACTIC POEMS

For Emma, Alyx and Penny —
another intergalactic trio!

ALIENS

Contents

ALIENS

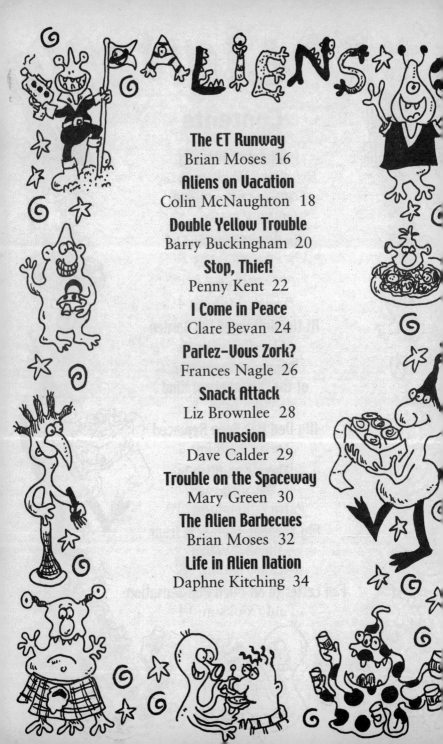

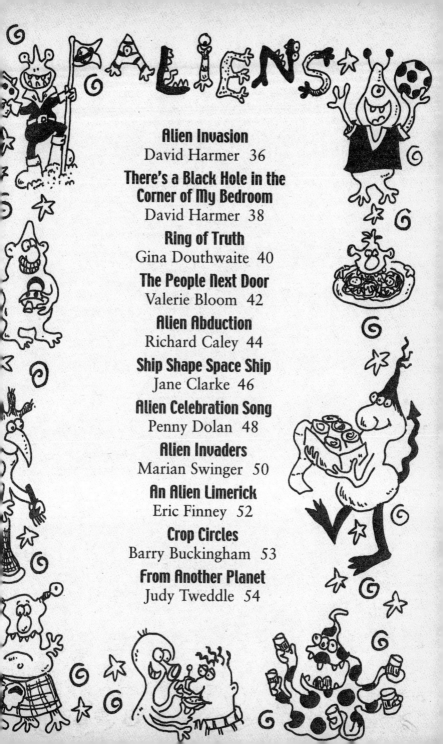

ALIENS

Mistaken Identity

I thought I'd seen a monster
From Outer Outer Space,
'Til Dad said, 'No it's just your mum
With a mud-pack on her face . . .'

Clive Webster

Aliens Strike Again!

Aliens stole my underpants.
They stole my sister's blouses.
They stole my mother's knickers.
They stole my father's trousers.

Aliens stole my grandma's teeth.
They stole my grandpa's socks.
They stole the baby's nappies.
(Mum kept them in a box.)

Aliens stole my brother's glasses.
They stole my uncle's shirt.
They stole my best friend's baseball cap.
They stole Aunt Susan's skirt.

These wicked thefts by aliens
Have really got to stop.
I wonder why they do it?
Perhaps they have a shop?

John Kitching

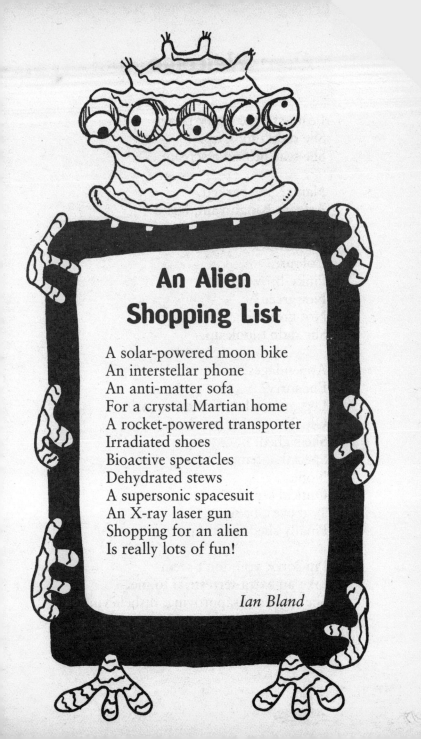

An Alien Shopping List

A solar-powered moon bike
An interstellar phone
An anti-matter sofa
For a crystal Martian home
A rocket-powered transporter
Irradiated shoes
Bioactive spectacles
Dehydrated stews
A supersonic spacesuit
An X-ray laser gun
Shopping for an alien
Is really lots of fun!

Ian Bland

Welcome

I came to the Entry Desk.
She didn't look up.
She was behind a screen.

Name? She barked.
Arfgam Banghwam, I said.
Planet of Origin?
Varglewark 3.
Colour?
Pinky-brown.
Not green?
Not green.
She didn't look up.

Appendages?
I'm sorry?
Legs, tentacles, tails etcetera.
Oh. Two arms, two legs.
She sighed.
Special antennae?
None.
Optical sensors?
Two eyes, brown.
Finally she looked up.

I'm sorry, you don't seem
Like an extra-terrestrial to me.
She looked disapproving, disbelieving.

I didn't want to disappoint her.
So I zapped her
With my third-brain zonic ray.
Bam!

She evaporated.
Satisfied? I asked.

Trevor Millum

NAME?

At the Bottom of the Garden

What's at the bottom of your garden?
A half-full sandpit covered in weeds;
A clump of dandelions spreading their seeds.

What's at the bottom of your garden?
A rusting bicycle against a wall;
A broken doll; an old football.

What's at the bottom of my garden?
An inter-galactic spacecraft refuelling station
Visited every night by faster than light machines
Cruising between the stars.
Of course, they put up their invisibility screens
Whenever I go near.

Well, it beats having fairies!

Alan Priestley

Supposed Encounter of the Alphabetical Kind

Alien Beings
Cunningly Descended Earthwards
From Galactic Holes,
In Jet-Kinetic-Laser
Masterships.

Not Offering Peace.

Quarrelsome Reptiles!

Savagely,
They Used Vaporising Weapons:

X – *Yonkers.*

ZAP ! ! !

Mike Jubb

My Dad Has Been Replaced

My dad
Has been replaced
By an alien.

He looks the same.
He sounds the same.
But he's not.

He has started
To do strange things:
The washing-up,
Making my pack-up,
Changing nappies.

And all this
Without being asked.

He gave me extra pocket money
And let me stay up late.
Was it a bribe
To keep me quiet?

I'm not sure
But even the dog
Is looking at him strangely.

My dad
Has been replaced
By an alien.

So far only I know this.

Trevor Millum

'There's an Alien in the Shed . . .'

Andy Gibbons said
there was an alien
in his grandad's shed.

He said it was lime green
with bulging purple eyes –
the scariest thing he'd seen.

He said it had three feet
electric shocking hair
and ate raw meat.

He said he'd touched its head
and pulled away
long slimy threads.

He said I wouldn't
dare to look –
and so I said I would.

With shaking hands
I opened the shed door.
Inside were spiders' webs
        a buzzing wasp
        a dried-up bumble bee

but nothing alien-like
that I could see.

Tough luck!
said Andy, grinning.
Guess it's gone for tea.

Patricia Leighton

My Teenage Brother is from Another Planet

He moons around.
He stares into space.
Red spots erupt
all over his face.

He still likes football
but dreams about girls.
He now inhabits
an alien world.

That's it! He's an alien!
It's official. It's true.
He's been taken over.
But what can I do?

It's too late to save him
so the plan must be
to prevent the same thing
happening to me.

Bernard Young

Fan Letter to an Alien Pop Sensation

Dear Stig Blurp,

I am thirteen eons old but I'm one of your biggest fans.
I have all your digital discs and interactive holograms.
You are the King of Spock and Roll, that's why I write
    this letter.
When I'm down I think of you and everything feels
    better.
You're the brightest star by far in our solar system
I've got three signed holographs and every day I've
    kissed them.
I love the way you cut your hair, especially on your
    chest.
Your song *'Baby Baby Grrrter Grax'* is the one I like
    the best.
At over eighteen kitos tall you really are so hunky
And with seven dancing feet your moonwalk is so
    funky.

I know you can't go everywhere when intergalactically
   famous
But next time you're on tour please come to Uranus.
I'd love to shake all your hands and kiss all those lips
My four knees turn to jelly when you swivel all your
   hips.
My hearts skip a beat or eight when you sing your song
Romantic lyrics dripping from your telescopic tongue . . .
'Zippult gortex tooger ooom unner pance eskree'
I sing them all the time and they mean all the world to
   me.
So send me something personal, please please write back
   soon.
You'll make this girl feel out of this world and over
   every moon.
Your appeal is universal so I know you'll understand
Just how much I love you.

Love from your greatest fan
X X Y X X X X Y

Paul Cookson

The ET Runway

*It is rumoured that in the Nevada Desert of America
there is a specially prepared ET Runway with welcome
messages permanently beamed into the sky to attract the
attention of low-flying extra-terrestrials. Meanwhile in a
back garden in Sussex . . .*

We've laid out what looks like a landing strip
in the hope of attracting an alien ship
and we've even managed to rig up a light
that will flash on and off throughout the night.
And we've spelt out 'welcome' in small white stones
and we've messed around with two mobile phones
till now they bleep almost continuously
and their signal plays havoc with next door's TV.
But it's for the greater good of mankind,
this could be a really important find.

And we're going to have an interstellar funday
when aliens land on *our* ET runway.
What a day it will be and what a surprise
when alien spacecraft snowflake the skies,
when strange beings christen our welcoming mat
to gasps of amazement, 'Just look at that!'
And to anyone out there listening in
the reception we'll give you is genuine:

We promise there'll be no limousines
to take you to tea with kings and queens.
No boring politicians from different lands,
no chatting on chat shows, or shaking of hands,
no scientists waiting to whisk you off

to investigate every bleep, grunt or cough.
It will only be us, just me and Pete
and a few friends from school you'll be happy to meet.
We could interview you for the school magazine:
'Do your spacecrafts run on gasolene?'

And we know it's not the desert in Nevada
but we really couldn't have tried much harder.
So if you can hear us, please make yourself known,
send us a signal, pick up the phone.
We've seen you out there, effortlessly gliding,
introduce yourselves now, it's time to stop hiding.

Brian Moses

Aliens on Vacation

They come from planets near and far,
Some big, some small, some quite bizarre.
Twinkle, twinkle, little star –
Aliens on vacation!

> They've read the brochures, booked hotels,
> Had their shots and said farewells.
> Run for cover! Ring them bells!
> Aliens on vacation!

Towards the Earth the pilot steers.
They've come to look for souvenirs,
Eat some pizza, drink some beers –
Aliens on vacation!

> If you stare, they'll start a fight.
> They sing rude songs and dance all night.
> They go to bed when it gets light –
> Aliens on vacation!

They hog the sunbeds round the pool,
Splash other guests and play the fool.
They write with spray-paint ALIENS RULE!
Aliens on vacation!

> They plunder, photograph and scour.
> Their spaceship has enormous power.
> It takes on board the Eiffel Tower . . .
> Aliens on vacation!

. . . From Israel, the Wailing Wall!
From London Town, the Albert Hall!
They take Mount Everest from Nepal . . .
Aliens on vacation!

        . . . Australia, they take Ayers Rock!
        From Scotland, they take Lomond Loch!
        From England, they take Big Ben's clock . . .
        Aliens on vacation!

 . . . From New York, the Empire State!
San Francisco, Golden Gate!
Never underestimate –
Aliens on vacation!

        With famous landmarks now just blanks,
        They check their oil and fill their tanks.
        They leave without a word of thanks –
        Aliens on vacation!

And as they leave, the aliens cheer
And chuck out empty cans of beer;
'We'll all be back again next year!' –
Aliens on vacation!

        There's just one thing they overlook:
        That when, next year, they try to book,
        The phone just might be off the hook –
        To aliens on vacation!

Colin McNaughton

Double Yellow Trouble

Our town lies in smouldering ruins –
just rubble and flickering fires.
And who is to blame?
Well, I'll tell you his name.
It's that new traffic warden called Squires.

You can't blame an alien for parking
on bright yellow lines painted double.
In Space, all the scout ships,
and small runabout ships,
can park where they like without trouble.

But Squires lost his cool in the High Street;
a UFO had parked rather careless.
He wrote out a ticket,
and then tried to stick it
on this bug-eyed creature, all hairless.

This upset the purple-skinned alien.
He puffed out a cloud of thick smoke.
And then came disaster –
he whipped out his blaster,
and flattened the town at a stroke!

Beware, then, of badly parked UFOs,
with bright flashing lights, gently humming.
Don't stop and deplore them.
Pass by and ignore them . . .
and hope Warden Squires isn't coming.

Barry Buckingham

Stop, Thief!

When we went to the cinema
to see the latest space movie
  we didn't expect a spacecraft
    to roar off the screen,
      brake sharply
        and hover over us
          as we cowered in our seats.

We didn't expect the spacecraft door
to flip open in a flash
  so that glaring lights
    blazed into our eyes
      and blinded us
        temporarily.

And we didn't expect
that whiplash tentacles
  would crack down,
    encircle our tubs of popcorn
      and whisk them up through
        the quickly closing door
          while crackles of weird alien laughter
            burst from the cinema loudspeakers.

And after all that,
we certainly didn't expect the spacecraft
    to cruise back onto the screen again
        and resume its part in the movie
            leaving us sitting open-mouthed
                with rumbling stomachs
                    and eyes popping in
                        astonishment.

Penny Kent

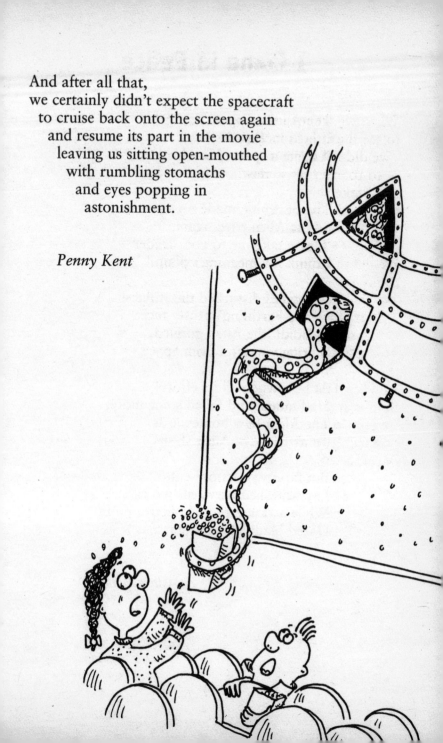

I Come in Peace

The Alien stepped forwards,
It held its flippers high,
'I come in peace,' it whistled,
'From somewhere in the sky.'

The Earthling made no answer,
So the Alien tried again,
'Please take me to your leader –
I think my meaning's plain.'

No smiles disturbed the stillness
Of the Earthling's frosty face.
'Behold!' the Alien gurgled,
'I bring you gifts from Space.'

At last, when all its efforts
Had failed, and failed some more,
The Alien flew homewards
To its friendly, Alien shore.

But far away, its presents
Lay squashed between two cars,
While a rather puzzled petrol pump
Gazed blankly at the stars.

Clare Bevan

Parlez-Vous Zork?

When our visitor from Zork arrived
I couldn't make out a word it said.
Nor could Mum.
But our baby could.

They got chatting straight away
And never stopped.
All day long it was,
MOOZLEWOB, DURDLE-DURDLE, PTHHHHH,
And stuff like that.
Such earnest conversations.

I hope when our baby learns English
He'll be able to remember,
And will tell me
What they were about.

Frances Nagle

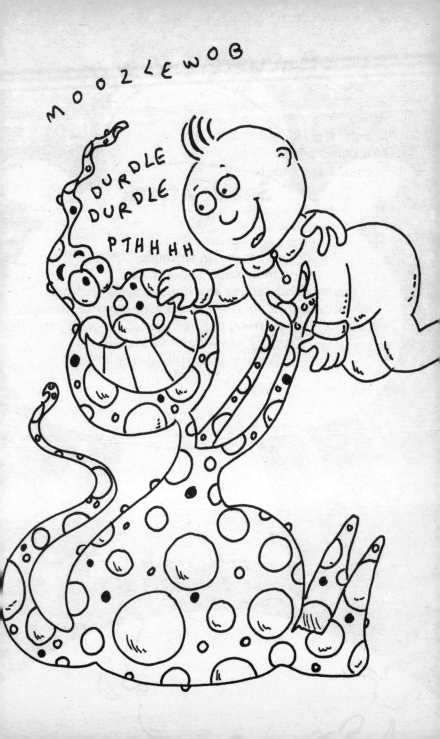

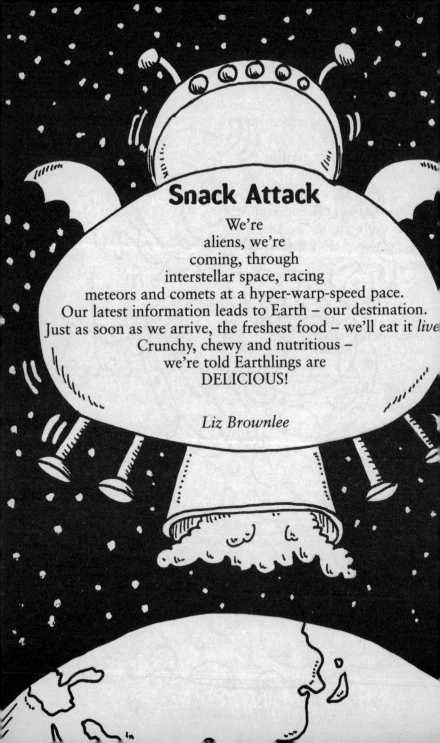

Snack Attack

We're
aliens, we're
coming, through
interstellar space, racing
meteors and comets at a hyper-warp-speed pace.
Our latest information leads to Earth – our destination.
Just as soon as we arrive, the freshest food – we'll eat it *live*
Crunchy, chewy and nutritious –
we're told Earthlings are
DELICIOUS!

Liz Brownlee

Invasion

When the aliens landed on earth
their mighty battle fleet
spread out in formation
along the shoreline of a sea.

When the aliens landed on earth
their commander stood on the shore
and claimed the planet. After all,
there was no resistance to their force.

When the aliens landed on earth
a boy, stepping over a puddle,
squashed them all.

Dave Calder

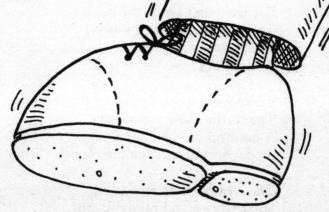

Trouble on the Spaceway

We started out from Neptune,
At helter-skelter speed,
For a Martian celebration,
On the planet Gannymede.

But we didn't know the misery,
That we were going to meet,
As we passed the thunder-buses,
And a flash new Venus jeep.

There were space-works on the orbital,
The traffic pulse was down,
A hold-up on the Pluto route,
And worm holes spinning round.

The weather was atrocious,
Solar storms and rainbow dust,
And the supernova Rover
Was growling fit to bust.

By the time we passed old Ceres,
Hurling rocks with all his might,
The craters in our camper-van
Were not a pretty sight.

We took the path to Jupiter,
A tried and tested rule,
But the camper-van began to squeal,
I'm running out of gruel!

So we left the super spaceway,
And took the autobahn,
And through the laws of retro-time,
Arrived where we began.

Mary Green

The Alien Barbecues

A heavenly pong that we just couldn't trace
has been drifting around up here in space,
till our saucers returned with wonderful news –
it's the smoke from your back garden barbecues.

They smell saucy, spicy and appetising,
scrumptious and luscious, quite tantalising,
delightful, delectable, delicious, it's true,
succulently savoury, nutritious too.

Now we've been sent to discover more
of this fast food formula that we can't ignore;
for we've cooked it ourselves and we can't get it right
and that's why we keep calling round every night.

It's so munchable, crunchable, truly scrummy,
gorgeous, mouth-watering, chewy and yummy.
It tickles our tastebuds, our tongues become tangled
but it still isn't right and our teeth have got mangled.

You see all we have fed on for many light years
are red planet slugs kebabbed on small spears
like the party sausage you eat from a stick
but we're telling you now, they're making us sick.

They're slimy, they're yucky, disgustingly green
the most revolting creatures we've ever seen.
They're stinky and vile with a vinegary taste,
gungey and gooey like smelly fish paste.

So please help us out, we're really uptight.
Tell us the secret, we'll get out of your sight.
We won't invade, we'll turn round and go
once you've told us all that we need to know.

And when we're quite sure that we've got it right
we'll invite you to Mars for a fantastic night.
Red planet slugs you just won't refuse
when they're grilled on our alien barbecues.

Brian Moses

Life in Alien Nation

Alien and Alienesse
Have a beautiful alienome,
Where they live with their alienildren
And their bright red aliengnome.

He is an alienologist
At the alienfirmary,
Finding cures for alienitis
In the local community.

Alienache is common,
Alienella is rare
But is spread by disease in alien eggs,
So owners take note – and BEWARE!

She is an alienobat,
Every morning she swings and she climbs.
Then after lunch she's an alienmum
Reading alienursery rhymes.

They speak in Alienanish,
They travel by alienar,
Their life in Alien Nation
Is alieneally bizarre!

Daphne Kitching

Alien Invasion

Zigblad The Great, Mighty Warlord of the planet Drob,
Grand King and High Emperor of the Fifteen Galaxies,
Dragon Slayer, Beast Killer, Destroyer of Monsters
landed firmly on the planet's surface, flourished
his Vorgle Blast Super Ray Gun that once smashed the
   dreaded Smigz,
the Mighty Sword of Trygarth which slew the Seven
   Headed Spangleglurk,
the Shield of Vambloot which protected him from harm,
the Ring of Skigniblick, which gave him all power
and standing fast the mighty warrior
spoke out loudly, his voice ringing like the Great Bell
   of Hootrim,
*I claim this planet and all its creatures for the Empire
   of Drob.*
*Have great fear of me and my warriors, tremble at our
   mighty voices.*

Unfortunately,
he was suddenly swallowed
by a passing magpie, who thought he was
a very juicy beetle.

David Harmer

There's a Black Hole in the Corner of My Bedroom

So far I have lost
six red pencils, sixteen football stickers,
a million paper clips,
twenty-seven toffees coated with fluff,
a balloon, nine biros, some bubble gum
and twelve marbles.

Last week
I lifted the carpet at the corner
and saw a swirling tunnel of blackness
wobbling into nothing.
I pushed away the clouds with a pencil
and there was a little planet
twirling like a tiny ball.

Now they visit me. They fly
red and blue pointed spaceships
covered in dazzling tiny wires.
They talk to me and say,
Thank you for the toffee-flavoured fluff –
we love all your presents.

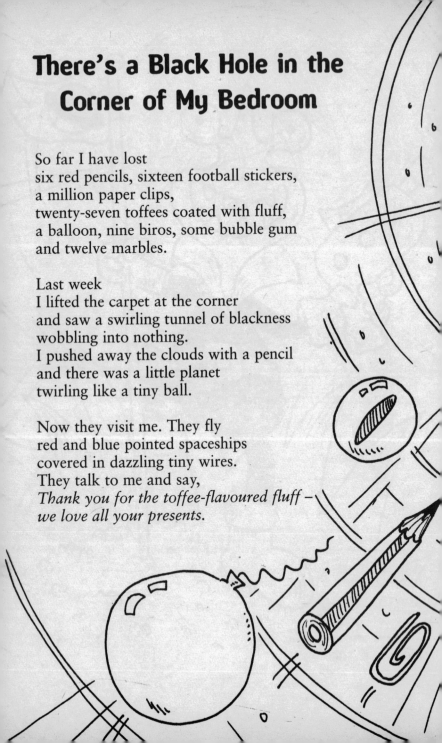

But they are puzzled by the marbles.
They never saw them. Perhaps
there is another black hole
inside my black hole
with another planet under that one
and so on forever.

My dad says there's a black hole
in his pocket every time we go shopping.
My mum says
I should be more careful with my things,
not keep losing them,
but you and I know different,
don't we?

David Harmer

Ring of Truth

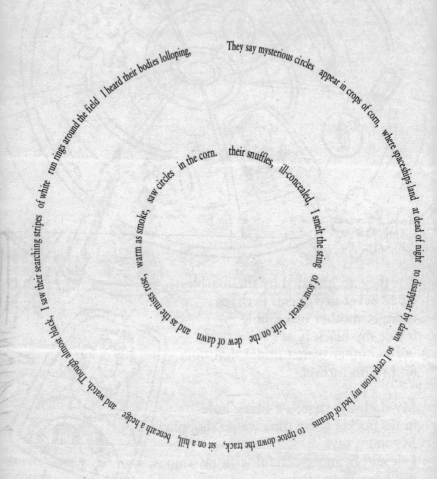

They say mysterious circles appear in crops of corn, where spaceships land at dead of night to disappear by dawn so I crept from my bed of dreams to tiptoe down the track, sit on a hill, beneath a hedge and watch. Though almost black, I saw their searching stripes of white run rings around the field I heard their bodies lolloping,

saw circles in the corn. their snuffles, ill-concealed, I smelt the sting of sour sweat drift on the dew of dawn and as the mists rose, warm as smoke,

Gina Douthwaite

The People Next Door

There are new people living next door,
They're as quiet as a comatose mouse,
We wouldn't have known there was anyone there,
But a blue light came on in the house.

And sometimes when they think no one's about,
A small head peeks out through the door,
But we never see any adult over there,
They all seem not much older than four.

Our dog used to chase rabbits in the garden next door,
But he hasn't gone near since they came,
The ducks in the pond flew away it seems,
And that's a pity, they were getting so tame.

And the rabbits that were always hopping next door
In their dozens have all disappeared,
In their garden, there isn't a bird or a bee,
Though we've got plenty, isn't that weird?

The vicar went over to welcome them in,
And now he is acting so odd!
If you ask him their names, or what they are like,
He'll just cross himself twice, smile and nod.

The postman who used to deliver their mail
Has gone away, no one knows where,
And that's such a shame because if anyone could
He would tell us what they're like over there.

The social worker went round to find out
Why the children weren't at school,
But we haven't seen her since, so I guess
She's probably visiting her mum in Blackpool.

Then we got a letter, pushed through the door.
Written on paper that just seems to glow,
Inviting us over for supper and games
Tonight at six. Do you think we should go?

Valerie Bloom

Alien Abduction

My brother claims that aliens
Abducted him last night
They beamed him straight up from his bed
Into their disc of light.

He says the 'things' that took him
Had bulbous heads of blue
And X-ray eyes that glowed bright red
When looking into you.

They had six scaly fingers,
Four legs and sixteen toes
He reckons they had silver teeth
Below a trumpet nose.

They carried out all kinds of tests
They measured height and girth
They used all sorts of instruments
We've never seen on Earth.

They looked into his stomach with
A type of 'space age' dart
They pulled out hair, they scraped off skin
Then analysed his heart.

He says he never felt a thing
Throughout he stayed quite calm
Even when they probed his head
And took apart his arm.

He says that when they'd finished
They showed him round their ship
Then beamed him straight back to bed
To carry on his kip.

I don't dismiss this story
It's possible I s'pose
Of course he'll never prove it
But then again who knows.

But if they came to study us
One question still remains
Why on Earth choose Trevor
And not someone with brains?

Richard Caley

Ship Shape Space Ship

Ship shot at by droids?
Been sucked into voids?
Or did space sickness strike all your crew?
If you're cratered by comets
And submerged in vomit
Let us make your ship shipshape for you.

We'll clean out your spark plugs
And vaporise space bugs,
Check your warp drive is faster than lightning.
We repair dents and holes
And replace toilet rolls
Because Outer Space can be frightening.

Alien ships huge or tiny
Will be shipshape and shiny.
Everyone's spreading the word –
If you want the best
Call S.S.S.S.
Our service is out of your world!

Jane Clarke

Alien Celebration Song

Usually sung with a great waving of tentacles.

Uhrghl pffflli nnng fu
Uhrghl pffflli nnng fu
Uhrghl pffflli zurrrrrrrghhh tzzzzt grrrk –
Uhrghl pffflli nnng fu!

Penny Dolan

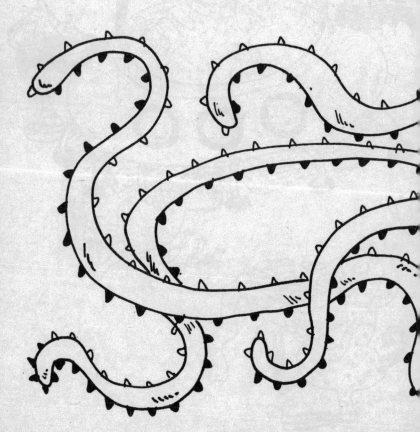

Alien Invaders

The space invaders slowed their ship,
and, weapons held in vice-like grip,
entered shuttles. Earthbound, they
landed on a rainy day
outside a little English town.
Ferocious aliens, green and brown
with small red eyes and sabre claws,
sharp fangs and slavering, drooling jaws
leapt, yelling into driving rain
and were washed, still yelling, down a drain.
They were but one centimetre high
so no one heard their angry cries.
Puddles formed. As people waded,
no one knew they'd been invaded.

Marian Swinger

An Alien Limerick

As on Red Planet, Mars, we alighted,
A very large banner we sighted.
'That's the answer,' I said,
'To why Mars is called "red"'.
It said MARTIANS ALL LOVE MAN UNITED.

Eric Finney

Crop Circles

It's a common belief that crop circles
are attempts by visitors from Space
to establish communications
with us of the Human Race.

But don't be fooled by the 'experts'
who think they know better than me.
Crop circles are done by UFO yobs . . .

It's alien graffiti, see?

Barry Buckingham

From Another Planet

When you first came,
we laughed at you
and called you sassenach.
As if you were from another planet.

Maggy Stewart pinched your Penguin.
Dougy McLean made jokes,
like 'Did you come intruder window?'
As if you didn't belong.

Mary McQueen pulled your plaits,
Jamie Souness called them ears,
and asked if they were your antennae.
As if you were a weirdo from outer space.

Hamish Bruce mocked your English accent,
Angus Dixon wouldn't stand behind you in the line.
Jean McLeod asked you for Mars Bars.
As if you were from Mars.

It was when we saw you standing by the radiator,
     crying, and
holding something in your hand, and
we knew that you had found Honey the Hamster, and
you said you wouldn't let her go until
we all stopped teasing and bullying you and
Jamie Souness was the first to say he was sorry and
Dougy McLean cried too because
he was the one who had left the cage open and
he was going to have to tell Mr Spink the headmaster
     that

it was his fault but he just said oh my god, and
you handed me Honey the Hamster because
it was my turn to feed her;

it was then that I really saw you
for the first time.

Judy Tweddle